CANDLEWICK PRESS

Candlewick Press, 99 Dover Street, Somerville, Massachusetts 02144. www.candlewick.com.
Printed in Shenzhen, Guangdong, China. 24 25 26 27 28 29 CCP 10 9 8 7 6 5 4 3 2

FIND OUT ABOUT
Animal Homes

Martin Jenkins

illustrated by

Jane McGuinness

Many different kinds of animals make homes to live in. They do this for all sorts of reasons: to stay warm and dry when it's cold and wet outside, to have somewhere safe to look after their babies, and to protect themselves from other animals that might eat them. Here are some of the homes that animals make . . .

There are **big** animals that have small **homes.**

A mother polar bear digs a cozy den in the snow just big enough for her and her cubs. It's warm and snug in there while it's freezing outside.

2

And small animals that have **big** homes, with air-conditioning and everything.

Termites live underground at the bottom of their mounds. Most kinds of termites are smaller than your little fingernail, but they can build mounds as tall as a bus—though it takes millions of them to do it! The way the mound is made keeps the air inside cool and fresh.

There are animals that make their homes out of sticks.

Many different kinds of birds make nests out of sticks to lay their eggs in. Storks make especially big nests. Often one pair uses the same nest year after year.

7

And ones that make them out of stones.

Young caddis flies, called larvae, live underwater. Some of them build homes out of tiny stones glued together with sticky stuff called silk that they make themselves. Each larva carries its home around with it.

And even some that make them out of spit. Yuck!

Edible-nest swiftlets live in Asia. They use their own saliva, or spit, to make nests. The saliva hardens and creates a safe place for the swiftlets' eggs and chicks.

There are animals that build homes
that last for years and years.

Prairie dogs live in big underground towns made of tunnels that they dig themselves.
The tunnels have rooms for sleeping, to use as nurseries, and for going to the bathroom.
The towns can be dozens of miles long and decades old.

And animals that build
a new one every day.

Every evening an orangutan makes a
comfortable nest out of branches and leaves
to sleep in that night. Sometimes
they'll build one for an afternoon
snooze as well!

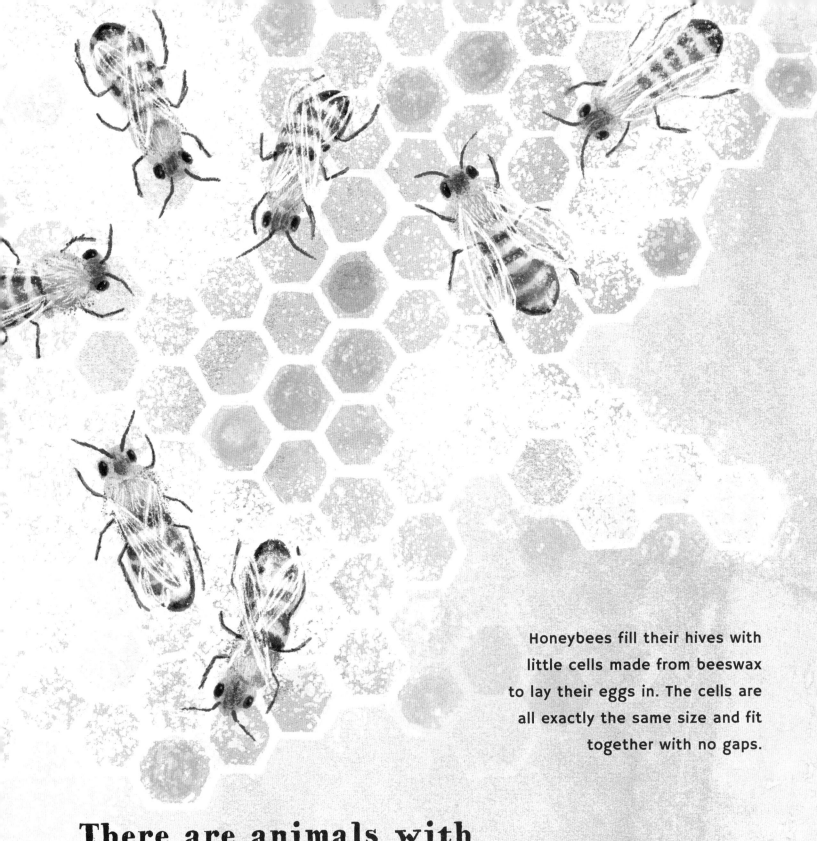

Honeybees fill their hives with little cells made from beeswax to lay their eggs in. The cells are all exactly the same size and fit together with no gaps.

There are animals with neat and tidy homes.

And animals with messy ones (like mine!).

Pack rats build their nests out of all sorts of stuff—mostly sticks and stones and garbage like plastic pots, rusty wire, and old bones.

There are animals with homes
that make a big impression.

Beavers dam up rivers and streams with mud, stones, and trees that they cut down. This creates big ponds that they build their dens, called lodges, in.

And animals with homes that you
can hardly see.

Some spiders build underground tunnels hidden beneath a trapdoor. When a small animal such as a cricket passes by, the trapdoor spider pushes open the door and leaps out to grab it.

And there are quite a few animals that don't make homes at all, but seem perfectly happy wherever they happen to be!

Reindeer live in the snowy north. They go on long journeys to escape the coldest part of the winter. Some of them walk more than 2,500 miles (4,000 kilometers) every year!

More About Animals and Their Homes

Most animals spend their lives living in one particular place that they know well, called a territory—it's their home. In that territory, they know where to find food and where to hide from animals that might hunt them. Often they try to keep other animals of the same kind away.

Animals sometimes change their territories to make life safer for themselves. Sometimes they dig burrows so that they have a place to hide. But the most common thing that animals do is build a nest, where they can look after their babies when they are young. Most birds do this, and a lot of insects, like termites and bees, make homes for their young, too.

Different insects use different things to make their homes. Honeybees make their own beeswax. Termites mostly use their own poop! They mix it with sand and spit so that it sets hard like concrete.

Not all animals have territories or homes. Animals that don't, like reindeer, usually live in big groups and travel around from place to place looking for food. They often come back to the same places year after year. Perhaps when they return, they recognize these spots and think of them as a kind of home, too.

INDEX